T0196029

Empowered
for
Wellbeing

Teresa Anne Palmer, MSN, RN, NPc

BALBOA.PRESS
A DIVISION OF HAY HOUSE

Balboa Press books may be ordered through booksellers or by contacting:

Balboa Press
A Division of Hay House
1663 Liberty Drive
Bloomington, IN 47403
www.balboapress.com
844-682-1282

Print information available on the last page.

ISBN: 978-1-9822-5377-6 (sc)
ISBN: 978-1-9822-5420-9 (e)

Library of Congress Control Number: 2020916588

Balboa Press rev. date: 02/24/2021

Contents

Introduction

I CHOSE TO write this book in the midst of uncertainty during an unprecedented time in history. A time when understanding how to take charge of our health and wellbeing is paramount.

Prologue

EACH INDIVIDUAL HAS the power to achieve and maintain good health and wellbeing. This personal power is present in each individual.

Each person has the following abilities:
The power to choose good health and wellbeing over illness and disease.
The power to remain confident, calm, and rationale regardless of the situation and or threat to one's health.
The power to build immunity and organ reserve
The power to partner in health and wellbeing
The power to choose courage over fear.
The power to live your best life.

Namaste: (I honor the light in you, which is the same light in me.)

What does it take to achieve and maintain good health?

NOT A LOT and it is not complicated. The truth is we have little education regarding how to take care of ourselves – and that is why I wrote this book. It is all about a simple daily practice of self-care. It is about using the knowledge and tools to become empowered for wellbeing.

I give you the tools needed and the ways to incorporate them in daily life. I give you a simple understanding of how stress contributes to the development of illness and disease and how it sabotages our ability to stay healthy.

It takes courage to live life regardless of the circumstances. When you know you are doing the best you can to maintain good health and wellbeing on the emotional, physical, and spiritual level, there is nothing to fear.

Part 1

Create Your Space Of Wellbeing

THE ABILITY TO achieve and maintain good health and wellbeing is dependent on the mind, body, and spirit working together. Often good health is believed to be physical-the absence of illness and disease. Health and disease are two sides of the same coin. Physical health is dependent on emotions and spirit.

In creating your space of wellbeing, attitude, perceptions, actions, and the ways the stressors of daily life are managed are as important to good health as sleep, diet, and exercise. The focus of this book is the spiritual aspects of good health. There will be no discussion on the importance of getting enough sleep, eating healthy, and daily movement/exercise. For decades we have been beaten over the head with these, and truth be told it has not made much of an impact on our ability to be well. The time has come to approach health and wellbeing from a different perspective.

In the year 2000, I had the privilege of participating in a medical mission to Romania. My training as a Nurse Practitioner was the medical model of "treating the symptoms of illness and disease"-not getting to the root cause of the ailments. I regarded myself as a "healer" as many in the health care profession do. Armed with my knowledge of treating symptoms with medication and diagnostic testing, I knew nothing about the role of who we are as individuals. How we live our daily lives determines how we are. My time in Romania opened a new world of how I would practice medicine from that time on.

Every morning before the clinic started, I would hear the children in the courtyard begin their day with song---a mantra that set the tone of the day and influenced their ability to be well. The lyrics are simple:

Every cell in my body is happy
Every cell in my body is happy

Every cell in my body is happy
Because I am at peace with myself

These simple words can have a powerful impact on wellbeing. Peace with oneself is contagious. How we act and treat ourselves determines how we influence others.

How Do We Attain Peace Within and How Does That Improve Our Health and Wellbeing?

Live from Your Heart

THE MANTRA I shared always ended the same. The children placed their hands over their hearts and felt the energy that radiates from the heart. The heart is the largest energetic field in the body, and because of that our emotions and feelings are felt by those around us. Our emotions, reactions, and actions directly influence others.

The heart is the center of emotions and reactions, and it connects to the brain via the Vagus nerve in the body's central nervous system. The Vagus nerve is responsible for activating the calm and peace within us. When the Vagus nerve is activated, the heart secretes a hormone ANP (atrial Natriuretic Peptide) more commonly known as the balance hormone. ANP regulates the heartbeat, lowers blood pressure, and synchronizes heart rate with breathing.

The Vagus nerve connects directly from the gut (abdomen) to the brain. This connection is part of the parasympathetic nervous system which maintains peace and calm and turns off the stress hormones responsible for "fight or flight".

Intention or Positive Thinking?

A familiar phrase is "to think positive". Thoughts are void of emotions. That is why positive thinking changes how one views or sees a situation, but it does not necessarily change the situation. Emotions are what change behavior by changing the energy. That is why intentions and intentional thinking are so powerful.

Intentions begin in the heart---our most powerful source of energy in the physical body. The heart can emit energy approximately six feet around it. That is why one person's emotional state affects those around them. Intentional thinking is thinking with a belief, and the heart processes that intention and belief. The heart sends the message to the brain, and a thought process is initiated that changes behavior and actions in accordance with the message of intent.

The heart emits energy and vibrations that affect those around them, and this energetic/vibrational influence is felt by others. If enough people have the same intentions---peace, harmony, social justice, love, compassion---then it becomes contagious, and others around begin to act in accord.

Living from the heart and acting with intention raise the energy and vibration allowing others to be influenced by it. The saying "be the change you want in the world" is about intentional thinking. Change begins with individual intention and can change the world. This is our opportunity to change the world to one of peace, harmony, love, compassion, and equality for all.

How Can Resilience Create
a Space of Wellbeing?

CHILDREN ARE OUR best teachers when it comes to
spirituality. Their resilience, forgiving nature, gratitude,
compassion, and the bonds they form with others create a
space of wellbeing.

Who we are determines how we are.

Somewhere in the process of growing up that spiritual
nature of seeing ourselves in others gets lost. When we
reclaim spirituality, we reclaim our personal empowerment
to achieve and maintain good health and wellbeing.

What effect does resilience, forgiveness, gratitude,
compassion, and relationships have on the ability to achieve
and maintain good health and wellbeing? They all allow
the immune system to function optimally, thus, increasing

immunity and decreasing chances of becoming ill. A healthy immune system fights off illness and disease. Additionally, *living from your heart may activate the thymus gland which plays a role in increasing the body's immune response.*

Resilience, forgiveness, gratitude, and compassion are the cornerstones of living from your heart. Our ability to maintain relationships and bond with others is proof we are all interconnected, and our individual actions affect the whole.

Resilience is the ability to bounce back from adversity. It is the understanding that things around us cannot always be controlled. It is "going with the flow". It is the acceptance of what is in the present. Resilience is not letting what happens adversely defeat us, rather make us stronger, learning from the experience.

How Can Forgiveness Impact Our Health?

Forgiveness is the most difficult concept to understand. The act of forgiving is often confused with forgetting. The ability to forgive another is an act of moving forward with one's life.

When we hold a grudge or refuse to let go of the pain and anger, we lose the ability to get on with life. This pain and anger eat away at body and soul depleting our immunity. Holding on to pain and anger only hurts oneself-often the other party has forgotten what happened or does not care about it. He goes on living his life. To free oneself from pain and anger, forgiveness is essential. In no way does that mean what happened was not important nor forgotten. It simply means the pain and anger are released, and the chains are broken that prevented life from moving forward. The act of forgiving allows the body and soul to heal. It returns the physical body to a state of balance, and the heart opens to peace.

Create your Space of Wellbeing Tool #1:

Sit quietly with eyes closed. Focus on the heart center. Envision a white ball of light. Feel the light warm your heart. Focus your attention on who/what you are having difficulty forgiving. Settle into any anxiety or fear that is evoked. Breathe into it and with each exhale feel it move outside you until it disappears. Now focus your attention on the white ball of light in your heart. Feel that ball of light expanding outside the heart to the pain, anger, and resentment holding you back. Watch as the white ball of light makes the pain, anger, and resentment disappear. You are left with peace, joy, and contentment-smile. Open your eyes.

What Positive Effects Do Gratitude, Compassion, and Social Interaction Have on Our Overall Wellbeing?

GRATITUDE IS AN essential tool for good health and wellbeing. Being grateful eliminates anger and resentment over what could or should have been. Negative thoughts and resentment lower the body's immunity and open the door to illness and disease. The act of being grateful allows for more abundance in life.

<u>Create your Space of Wellbeing Tool #2:</u>

> *Keep a gratitude journal. Each morning upon awakening think of one thing for which you are grateful. Write it down. Throughout the day remind yourself of what you are grateful for. This is a powerful practice---keeping a daily journal of gratitude.*

Compassion is the ability to see ourselves in others. Compassion extends to all beings and is the foundation for everything. Compassion and empathy are two separate things and are often confused. Compassion connects to people's feelings whereas empathy permits people to understand the emotions others are feeling. When we take on another's feeling, the risk is that these feelings may overwhelm and cause physical illness which can lead to the development of disease. Compassion is about caring, concern, and doing what can be done to help. Compassion is opening our hearts to all beings.

Create your Space of Wellbeing Tool #3:

Clearing the energy. At the end of the day it is important not to hold on to any energy that can linger as a result of practicing compassion. Sit quietly in a comfortable position and close your eyes. Imagine a white light at the top of your head. Watch as this light surrounds you with peace and tranquility. Open your eyes.

Building and Maintaining Strong Interpersonal Relationships is essential for our survival.

We were meant to be in connection to all beings and all creation. No man is an island is a popular phrase, and one we need to heed. Social isolation damages our health, mental wellbeing, and spiritual wellbeing.

How often do you hear of someone dying because either their spouse/significant other died recently or because they were socially isolated? Social isolation leads to depression, and depression often leads to death or suicide. Physically, a high level of stress associated with social isolation is a contributing factor to the development of heart disease, high blood pressure, diabetes, and dementia.

Create your Space of Wellbeing Tool #4:

Stay connected to friends and/or family. Call and talk to them at least once a week if you are unable to see each other physically. Otherwise, arrange to get together in person at least once a week. Joining group activities is another way to connect to others. What hobbies or social activities do you enjoy? Find out where these things are in your community or nearby and join. Make yourself available to others; volunteer work is another way to connect with others.

If social isolation is unavoidable due to illness or mobility issues, using technology is a good way to communicate and connect with others. Social platforms, such as face to Face calling, Zoom, Skype, and Facebook can keep you interconnected.

How we live our lives on a day to day basis incorporating resilience, gratitude, forgiveness, compassion, and staying in relationships with others has a positive effect on our ability to be well physically, emotionally, and spiritually.

Who we are determines how we are.

How Does Perception Influence Health? Our Thoughts and Feelings Become our Reality

PERCEPTION IS ALL about the reality we create. If we see ourselves as loving, kind, compassionate, our perception of the world is of abundance. Abundance promotes our ability to feel empowered.

If one perceives reality as one of scarcity never having enough, then feelings of powerlessness will prevail. Fear is a response to feeling that one's survival is at risk. It is a response that served us well in primitive times when the threat of survival was real. The brain would respond appropriately, sending the signals of "fight or flight". The body would react immediately. The stress hormones of adrenalin and epinephrine rushed into the bloodstream increasing heart rate, respirations, and blood pressure. Blood was directed to the extremities for a quick getaway from the threat. There was no time to think--react quickly and run was the message. It was all about saving one's self-survival.

As human beings evolved, the brain still remembered the threat of survival modality. The brain does not have the ability to decipher real fear (threat to survival) from the "perception" of fear (reactive/emotional response).

When "perception of fear" becomes the norm, then the brain remains in fight or flight mode, and the result is the state of chronic stress. Stress is a contributing factor to illness and disease which will be discussed later.

Besides one's own self-doubting perception of reality causing fear, events outside of our control trigger the same reaction. During COVID-19 misinformation and hyped media response sent many to grocery stores hoarding food and paper products. Social distancing and the threat of the virus made many afraid of any contact with others, fanning the flames of a world already experiencing social isolation from "stay at home "ordinances.

Fear disrupts the body's immune system and directly affects the ability to stay healthy at a time when it is most imperative to do so. Fear can be tamed and managed. One of the most effective ways to do this is to work with our body's natural force---the chakras.

Understanding the Chakras

The chakras are concentrated centers of energy in the body. The word chakra is derived from Sanskrit meaning wheel or disk. Chakras are depicted as spinning wheels of energy. These energetic wheels are important because each chakra corresponds with a gland or organ in the human body. The chakras align midline along the spine and nervous system. When the chakras are balanced and in perfect alignment, the flow of energy throughout the body is unobstructed and the body maintains balance.

The subtle energy of the chakras plays a role in hormone balance which is an essential part of achieving and maintaining good health and wellbeing.

The first chakra is the root chakra located at the base of the spine. This chakra is associated with survival and security. To manage fear is the work of the first chakra. Fear is about not feeling secure, grounded, or safe. When the body is grounded, fear is abated.

The second chakra is the sacral chakra located in the pelvis. This chakra is associated with sex hormones, creation, creativity, and passion. It is about creating new ways of thinking and/or doing things. The second chakra is also about the story we tell ourselves and the world.

Our story is based on our beliefs, perceptions, values, and experiences. Since each individual is the author of their story, the script can be rewritten at any time.

The third chakra, the solar plexus, is in the abdominal area below the naval. It is associated with our gut and adrenal glands. This is our center of personal power---the ability to reduce and manage stress (the adrenal glands) and to develop and utilize intuition or intuitive sense---gut feeling.

The fourth chakra is the heart chakra and is associated with love, compassion, and relationships. The heart chakra stimulates the thymus gland, which boosts immunity and is crucial for good health and wellbeing.

The fifth chakra, the throat chakra, is associated with our ability to communicate---to speak our truth and stand up for truth, justice, and equality. The thyroid gland is associated with the throat chakra and this hormone governs metabolism and the body's utilization of energy.

The sixth chakra is the third eye and is located between the eyebrows. It is known as the guidance chakra. The sixth chakra is about seeing the bigger picture-looking beyond what can only be seen with the naked eye. It is associated with the pituitary gland, which governs how the hormones keep the body in balance to function optimally.

The seventh chakra is the crown chakra located at the crown of the head. This chakra is often referred to the chakra of enlightenment. In practical terms, one is able to use rationale thought and acts with love, caring, and compassion. This chakra is associated with the pineal gland which is responsible for maintaining balance (homeostasis) of the other glands. It also regulates melatonin, sleep cycle, and serotonin (promotes stable mood).

Create your Space of Wellbeing Tool #5:

Sit quietly in a comfortable position.

Feel your buttocks and hips beneath you, supporting you as you sit. Close your eyes and imagine a small spinning disk of white light at the base of your spine. Feel that spinning disk radiate into the ground, anchoring you firmly to the earth. Feel the earth support you. You are secure and grounded. Now think about your fear(s). What are you afraid of? Take that/those fear(s) and place them inside the spinning disk of white light. Watch as your fear(s) becomes smaller and smaller until it disappears. The root chakra has absorbed this negative energy and replaced it with security, safety, and grounding.

To better understand fear and how it impacts our ability for health and wellbeing, it is necessary to understand the brain's connection to the heart.

The Heart Has A Brain: Understanding The Mind/ Body Connection

THERE WAS A time when "thinking" was the sole function of the brain. Then science discovered the heart has a brain---an intrinsic network of neurotransmitters that connect to the brain via the Vagus nerve located in the spinal cord. In fact, the heart sends more information to the brain than the brain to the heart. Additionally, these neurotransmitters are responsible for the viability of the heart muscle, the heart rate, and the heart rhythm.

How does the heart "think"?

Our emotions---joy, contentment, fear anxiety, etc.---are processed by the heart and then messaged to the brain via the Vagus nerve. If emotions are processed as calm and feeling good, the heart secretes Oxytocin (associated with empathy, trust, and love), telling the brain that all is well. The parasympathetic nervous system is activated and signals the release of Endorphins (the body's natural pain reliever), dopamine (associated with pleasurable sensations, learning and memory), and serotonin (which regulates mood, sleep appetite, learning ability, and memory).

When the Vagus nerve activates the parasympathetic nervous system, the heart secretes a substance Atrial Natriuretic Peptide (ANP) known as the balance hormone.

When the heart processes what we are feeling as "dangerous", the brain is sent the message to activate the sympathetic nervous system "fight or flight-signaling the release of the stress hormones adrenalin, epinephrine, and cortisol. It is these hormones that wreak havoc with the physical body contributing to the development of illness and disease.

The Vagus nerve is the mind/body connection serving as a conduit between the heart-brain and every organ, muscle, and cell in the body.

Create your Space of Wellbeing Tool #6:

Connect to Your Heart. This meditation allows you to live from your heart, not your head. The heart is fearless.

When you connect to your heart, you connect to your life force, and in doing so you connect to the peace within you---which is essential for good health and wellbeing.

Sit in a comfortable position in a quiet space without distractions.

Inhale deeply and slowly and exhale the same. Repeat 2 more times.

Place both hands over your heart. Feel your heart beating. Feel the energy pulsating, flowing throughout your body, nourishing every part of your being. Now direct the flow of energy to your hands and arms. Feel the warmth and calm. Extend your arms outward reaching out to everyone and everything---to your energy, your love reaching those who need it, your peace, calm, and compassion extended to those in need. Place your hands back over your heart. This energy, this beating heart, is your life force---the divine within you. It is meant to be shared. Inhale and exhale. When you are ready open your eyes.

I explained the chakras in simple terms and would like to expand on discussion of the third chakra---the solar plexus and the fifth chakra---the throat as it relates to living from your heart.

The third chakra---the solar plexus---is where our personal power resides (the power to achieve and maintain good health and wellbeing). This power needs to connect to the heart---the fourth chakra---(standing in one's truth) and the throat---the fifth chakra (speaking one's truth). The Vagus nerve acts as a bridge connecting the three chakras. It is only when an individual is confident in his ability to stand up for his beliefs and articulate what his needs are that his personal power is activated.

Create Your Space of Wellbeing Tool #7: Connect to your personal power.

Each of us has the power to heal through not only our actions but through our ability to communicate and partner in our health and wellbeing. This simple meditation activates your personal power. Sit comfortably, placing your hands on your abdomen. Visualize a white whirling energetic light just above your navel. Feel your personal power as it warms your hands. Now move your hands to your heart grounding that white light, that energy-your personal power in your heart and hands. Move your hands to your throat. Feel the energy giving you the power to speak your truth.

Nothing or no one can take your personal power from you.

Part 2

Creating Your Space of Wellbeing with Meditation and Intentional Breathing

IN PART 1 I talked about *living from your heart* though resilience, compassion, forgiveness, gratitude, and building/maintaining strong interpersonal relationships. Wellbeing starts with the creation of an internal landscape cultivated with love for oneself and others. This is the first step in self-empowerment to take charge of your health and wellbeing.

Meditation and intentional breathing build on that foundation of health and healing because they are the backbone for stress reduction and management. Since about

70% of chronic disease are stress related, the power to be healthy and well is in our control.

Meditation is a simple practice that requires nothing other than being in a quiet place and focusing on breathing for 10 minutes-morning and evening. Meditation benefits the mind, body, and spirit. It balances the body systems and alleviates anxiety, depression, and pain. It improves focus and concentration, memory, learning, and perception. Meditation lowers blood pressure, regulates heart rate and breathing, decreases metabolism, and boosts immunity. I call meditation the gold standard for achieving and maintaining good health and wellbeing.

How Meditation Changes the Brain

MEDITATION ENHANCES THE conductivity between the various centers of the brain, allowing each center to work together. The result is a brain that is resilient by having the ability to build new connections.

Mediation strengthens the Pons---the area of the brain that regulates sleep, facial expressions, processing sensory input, and basic physical functioning.

A daily practice of meditation shrinks the Amygdala, known as the "primitive" brain, which is associated with producing fear, anxiety, and the stress response---fight or flight.

Meditation affects the Prefrontal Cortex, which is the area of the brain responsible for fueling negative emotions and enhancing the ability to make rational decisions.

By shifting focus from "me" to "we", meditation affects the Temporo Parietal Junction. This area of the brain is associated with developing empathy and compassion.

Thrive not Survive

Why do some of us thrive while others survive? When we look at the COVID-19 pandemic, many lives were lost---not only by the virus, but by our reaction to what was going on. Fear kept many people from living. Yes, they existed, but fear kept them in lockdown. It takes courage to live and thrive. A daily practice of meditation can bridge the gap between fear and courage, thriving instead of surviving.

Meditation turns off the sympathetic nervous system response of fight or flight. Meditation allows access to the higher intelligence centers of the brain and integrates rational thinking. This ability to put aside fear and panic allows one to see the bigger picture. There are always "unknowns"; often waters are unchartered as life unfolds. When calm and inner peace take charge, then any difficulty unforeseen circumstance can be dealt with effectively.

It's All About the Breath

There is little or no attention paid to breathing, yet without breath there is no life. Breathing occurs automatically without having to think about it or pay it any attention. However, to achieve and maintain good health and wellbeing, it is essential to breathe correctly and with intention.

The breath is referred to as the "life force". Inhaling air into the lungs oxygenates every cell, tissue, and organ in the physical body. With each exhalation, carbon dioxide is removed. The physical body has a cycle of breathing in and out.

Intentional or deliberate breathing plays a role in stress reduction by activating the parasympathetic nervous system. Even under minimal stress more air is taken into the lungs when breathing is intentional. Being aware of inhaling and exhaling slowly and deeply is a form of meditation and relaxation.

Create Your Space of Wellbeing Tool #8: Intentional Breathing

Inhale slowly and deeply to the count of 8. Feel the breath as it enters your lungs. If comfortable, hold the breath to the count of 4. Exhale slowly to the count of 8. Feel the tingling sensation in your body as you breathe

TERESA ANNE PALMER, MSN, RN, NPc

slowly, deeply, and intentionally. Do this throughout each day.

There are several methods of controlled breathing that are worth mentioning. The first method is *alternate nostril breathing. This breathing technique utilizes both nostrils to stimulate both sides of the brain-the right side and the left side. At any given time, although it appears that inhalation involves both nostrils, in reality one nostril dominates the breathing cycle for several hours.*

Create Your Space of Wellbeing Tool #9: Alternate Nostril Breathing

Begin by sitting comfortably. Inhale slowly to the count of 8. If able, hold the breath to count of 4. Then slowly exhale to the count of 8. With that completed, take your right hand and pinch the right nostril closed with your thumb. Breathe in slowly to the count of 8 through your left nostril. Pinch your left nostril closed with your first finger. If able, hold the breath to the count of 4. Now release your right nostril with your thumb and exhale slowly to the count of eight. Close your left nostril with your first finger inhaling slowly through the right nostril to count of 8. Pinch both nostrils closed with thumb and first finger and hold to count of 4. Release the left nostril and exhale slowly to the count of 8. Repeat alternating right and left nostril for 8 cycles.

Another method of breathing is Kapalabhati (kah-pah-luh-BAH-tee) or skull shining breath as it is often referred to as. This breathing technique consists of short, powerful exhales with gentle inhales. Kapalabhati breathing is a cleansing technique that helps detoxify all the systems in the physical body.

Create Your Space of Wellbeing Tool #10:

Sit in a comfortable position and take a deep breath in. As you exhale, contract your abdomen to force the air out. You can place your hand on your belly to feel the abdominal muscles contract. As the breath is quickly released from your abdomen, the inhale should happen automatically. One round is 20 breaths. In the beginning start with 5 and then 10 and when comfortable with this breathing advance to 20 breaths. As you do this practice, you will feel sensations throughout the physical breathing. If you have any lung conditions or breathing concerns, consult your health care provider before beginning this practice.

When Is Stress Beneficial?

STRESS DOES SERVE a purpose when there is a dangerous and/or life-threatening situation. Under these circumstances, the stress response (flight-or-fight response), the rapid release of the stress hormones-adrenalin, epinephrine, and cortisol act in unison to provide the human body with the necessary survival tools. Adrenalin and epinephrine shunt blood from the stomach, kidneys, liver, and pancreas to the extremities and brain. The ability to run and think is critical to survive danger.

In the face of danger, the heart beats faster to pump more blood and the blood pressure rises. More oxygen is needed by the heart and lungs; breathing becomes more rapid and shallow. Clotting factors are released into the bloodstream allowing the blood to clot faster (in case of injury). Cortisol is secreted by the adrenal glands to increase blood sugar to the muscles to be used as energy. The cells begin to store fat in case extra energy (fuel) is needed. As blood sugar levels rise, insulin production decreases in response to cortisol. Cortisol also constricts the arteries in the heart (coronary arteries) to aid the heart in pumping blood faster.

High blood sugar, the shunting of blood from the kidneys, liver, and stomach (decreasing urination and affecting the elimination of bodily waste products), temporary halting of food digestion, increased blood pressure, rapid pulse, shallow rapid breathing, and increased ability for blood clotting are all life saving measures of the stress response.

The reason for this discussion about stress management is that stress has become a chronic state of how individuals function on a daily basis. We are stuck in the flight-or-fight response and the resulting cascade of disequilibrium that threatens our ability for good health and wellbeing. In other words, we become powerless and at the mercy of stress's destructive forces.

Stress and Organ reserve

"The function of protecting and
developing health must rank
even above that of restoring it when it is impaired."
Hippocrates

ORGAN RESERVE IS the capacity that the human body can function beyond the baseline functionality. When the physical body has optimum organ reserve, this reserve allows the individual to overcome the physical taxation associated with illness, injury, traumatic assault on the body. In other words, it is directly related to the ability to recover from illness, disease, virus and bacterial infections, and life-threatening illness.

When the physical body is constantly under stress and no measures are taken to reduce, manage and eliminate stress, there is little to no organ reserve. By creating a space of wellbeing with the tools I share, there will be optimum organ reserve. *An individual's ability to be in control of stress is being empowered to take charge of his health and wellbeing at an extremely critical level.*

Overview Of How Stress
Affects The Physical Body

APPROXIMATELY 70% OF all medical visits to health care providers are stress related. Heart Disease, Diabetes, Gastro-Intestinal conditions, and autoimmune disorders are examples of the toll that stress takes on the body. The ways stress impedes the ability to achieve and maintain good health and wellbeing are the following:

High blood sugar causes impaired insulin production and utilization as the pancreas struggles to regulate blood sugar contributing factors for the development of diabetes. Although the exact mechanism is unclear, it is theorized that the excessive or constant secretion of cortisol renders the cells insulin resistant.

High blood pressure, the constriction of the coronary arteries, and a heart beating faster increase the burden on the heart muscle, which results in heart disease---especially heart failure.

Impaired digestion of food and essential nutrients contribute gastrointestinal disorders.

Disruption in the kidney and liver's ability to remove waste products allow for toxins to accumulate in the blood.

Increasing the blood's ability to clot more quickly, changes the viscosity of the blood making it thicker which may contribute to the development of Coronary Artery Disease. (CAD). And if these are not reasoning enough to manage stress, there is more.

The Culprit is Cortisol

CORTISOL, THE HORMONE secreted in response to stress, *wreaks havoc*. Cortisol is produced and regulated by the adrenal glands. During times of stress the adrenal glands secrete an excess amount of cortisol in preparation for the flight or fight response. Excessive cortisol causes *weight gain* and making weight loss difficult to achieve. Cortisol mobilizes triglycerides (fat) to the visceral fat cells located deep in the abdomen, which is responsible for the development of the potbelly and spare tire. Adding insult to injury, cortisol decreases the amount of sugar the body stores in the cells. The cells then send a message to the brain – we need more energy-send us food-Increased food intake-weight gain

Additionally, it is theorized that cortisol may also bind to the hypothalamus receptors located in the brain. The hypothalamus controls appetite. The binding of the cortisol to the receptors may *increase the appetite signal,* resulting in increased caloric consumption, hunger, and resulting weight gain. Excessive secretion of cortisol constricts the arteries that provide blood flow to the brain and may be a risk factor for dementia. Initially cortisol reduces the body's inflammatory response- allowing the immune system to function properly. However, when cortisol is over secreted, as in the state of chronic stress, it eventually suppresses the immune system.

The immune system dysfunctions, resulting in an increase in inflammation in the body cells and tissues. Cortisol is no longer effective in lowering the inflammatory response. This state of increased inflammation contributes to the development of autoimmune diseases such as Rheumatoid arthritis, lupus, and fibromyalgia.

Chronic stress (cortisol over secretion) disrupts the immune system resulting in an increase in inflammation in the body's tissues and cells and related autoimmune diseases. This *inflammation* plays a critical role in Coronary Artery disease and Myocardial infarctions (heart attack). High blood pressure, elevated cholesterol, and cigarette smoking all contribute to the development of plaque in the arteries of the heart. This plaque formation narrows and blocks the arteries, which is known as Coronary Artery Disease. A

Myocardial Infarction, or heart attack occurs when a piece of this plaque breaks off the walls of the artery or arteries stopping blood flow to the heart and causing damage to the heart muscle. In the presence of inflammation, the body responds by attacking the plaque in the arteries by releasing inflammatory fighting chemicals called macrophages into the arteries to attack the plaque. This turbulent, foaming action of the macrophages can cause a piece of the plaque to break off, block the artery and /or arteries, resulting in a myocardial infarction.

Inflammation has become an important aspect of preventative cardiac care. Inflammatory markers are measured in the blood. The higher the values are, the greater the risk of a myocardial infarction. The cardiac risks associated with inflammation are so important research is currently underway to find ways of reducing the damage the inflammatory process causes.

Eventually under long periods of stress the adrenal glands are unable to sustain the production of cortisol. This drop in cortisol production causes a domino effect involving the master hormone Pregnenolone and the Thyroid gland.

Pregnenolone is a master hormone and is responsible for the production of Estrogen and Progesterone. In addition, Pregnenolone is often used as a medication or supplement to improve cognitive and memory function. When the adrenal glands are overworked and their ability to continue to secrete cortisol wanes, Pregnenolone steps in and produces cortisol. Known as the Pregnenolone "steal", instead of making Estrogen, Cortisol is made instead. This results in a deficit of Estrogen to be utilized by the body. A deficit in Estrogen is a contributing factor to irregular menstrual cycles, mood swings, and infertility.

As the adrenal glands are overworked and overstressed, the fluctuations in cortisol affect the thyroid gland. As the thyroid gland struggles to regain homeostasis (balance) in the body, it slows down the metabolism causing more weight gain and making it extremely difficult for weight loss.

Additionally, stress directly affects the thyroid gland by disrupting the thyroid gland to function normally. The thyroid gland is responsible for regulating metabolism and the rate and strength of the heartbeat, raising the oxygen concentration in the body, regulating body temperature, and aiding in growth and development during childhood.

Two hormones are secreted by the thyroid gland: T3 (triiodothyronine) and T4 (thyroxine). T3 is the active hormone and T4 is the inactive hormone, that is converted to the active hormone T3. Under stress, there is a reduction in the amount of T4 that converts to T3. As a result, the thyroid gland must work harder to produce enough T3. This strain on the thyroid gland is a contributing factor to the development of thyroid disease.

Stress has a direct effect on the cells in the body causing them to divide faster than the normal cycle of cell division. This rapid division of cells is a contributing factor to accelerated aging and possibly a link to the development of some cancers.

The ability for the body to age naturally and with grace is hindered by how stress affects the Telomeres. Telomeres are sheaths of DNA that are located on the end of chromosomes. Their function is to protect the genetic data contained in the cells. Rapid division of the cells in the body shorten the telomeres leading to an acceleration in the aging process.

Create Your Space of Wellbeing: Tool #11:

A daily practice of Meditation and some form of daily exercise have been effective in preserving the length of the telomeres and may aid in prevention of rapid cell division.

The Afterword

Empowered for Wellbeing is:

1) Choosing to live from your heart
2) Having a daily practice of meditation
3) The practice of intentional breathing
4) Recognizing and managing stress
5) Partnering in achieving and maintaining good health and wellbeing by being actively involved in healthcare decisions

YOU HAVE THE POWER